D0051706

Implementing Project-Based Learning

Suzie Boss

Solution Tree | Press

a division of
Solution Tree

555 North Morton Street
Bloomington, IN 47404
800.733.6786 (toll free) / 812.336.7700
FAX: 812.336.7790

email: info@solution-tree.com
solution-tree.com

Printed in the United States of America

19 18 17 16 15   2 3 4 5

Library of Congress Cataloging-in-Publication Data

Boss, Suzie.
  Implementing project-based learning / by Suzie Boss.
      pages cm
  Includes bibliographical references.
  ISBN 978-1-942496-11-3 (perfect bound) 1. Project method in teaching.
I. Title.
  LB1027.43.B64 2015
  371.3'6--dc23
                              2015009170

Solution Tree
Jeffrey C. Jones, CEO
Edmund M. Ackerman, President

Solution Tree Press
President: Douglas M. Rife
Associate Acquisitions Editor: Kari Gillesse
Editorial Director: Lesley Bolton
Managing Production Editor: Caroline Weiss
Copy Chief: Sarah Payne-Mills
Copy Editor: Jessi Finn
Proofreader: Elisabeth Abrams
Text Designer: Rachel Smith
Cover Designer: Rian Anderson

Acknowledgments

Sincere thanks to the teachers who took time to unpack their thinking about project-based learning. Their examples and insights are invaluable for helping us understand how to design projects that engage and challenge digital-age learners.

In particular, I'd like to thank Armin Heurich, Eric Clause, Gail Shatkus, Heather Wolpert-Gawron, Milko Wagner, and Raleigh Werberger. Robert Kolvoord and Stewart Kirkpatrick offered important insights about the value of geospatial thinking. Harshil Parikh helped me understand the importance of data literacy for 21st century learners.

To the team at Solution Tree, thank you for the invitation to contribute to this series.

Visit **go.solution-tree.com/technology** to access materials related to this book.

Table of Contents

About the Author

 **Suzie Boss** is a writer and educational consultant who focuses on the power of teaching and learning to transform communities. She has developed programs for nonprofit organizations that teach youth and adults how to improve their communities with innovative, sustainable solutions. She has also introduced project-based learning (PBL) strategies to after-school providers to enrich the experiences of youth at risk.

She is a member of the National Faculty of the Buck Institute for Education, an international resource for best practices in PBL. She is a frequent conference presenter and consults with schools around the globe interested in shifting from traditional instruction to technology-rich, project-based learning. She has also worked with educators online, facilitating webinars and extending professional development events.

She is the author of several books on education and innovation, including *Bringing Innovation to School: Empowering Students to Thrive in a Changing World*, *Reinventing Project-Based Learning: Your Field Guide to Real-World Projects in the Digital Age*, and *Real-World Projects: How Do I Design Relevant and Engaging Learning Experiences?* She is a regular contributor to Edutopia and the *Stanford Social Innovation Review*, and her work has appeared in a wide range of other publications, including *Educational Leadership*, *Principal Leadership*, the *New York Times*, the *Huffington Post*, and *Education Week*.

Suzie holds a bachelor of arts degree in communications from Stanford University.

To learn more about Suzie Boss's work, visit her blog *Reinventing Project-Based Learning* (http://reinventingpbl.blogspot.com), and read her Edutopia contributions (www.edutopia.org/users/suzie-boss). Connect with her on Twitter @suzieboss.

To book Suzie Boss for professional development, contact pd@solution-tree.com.

Introduction

If you follow the headlines about the state of the U.S. education system, it's easy to feel discouraged. International comparisons show American students lagging behind their peers in South Korea, Singapore, Finland, and many developed countries in measures of academic achievement. Fewer than three in ten Americans think high school graduates are prepared for college, and fewer than two in ten think their grads are ready for the workforce (Gallup, 2014). Teacher turnover is portrayed as yet another symptom of a broken system and dispirited teaching force.

Even worse, students themselves may be abandoning their youthful optimism. While 54 percent of students describe themselves as hopeful about the future, 32 percent say they feel "stuck," and 14 percent are outright discouraged (Gallup, 2014). Although student engagement still runs high in the early grades, it falls steadily the longer students spend in school (Fullan & Donnelly, 2013).

Get past these negative sound bites and into actual classrooms, however, and you can find plenty of cause for optimism about today's youth and their readiness to tackle challenges. That's especially true in schools that leverage project-based learning (PBL) strategies, combined with ready access to technology.

In schools across the United States and internationally, I regularly encounter students who are working to improve their neighborhoods, address global inequities, and design innovations that will improve their families' and communities' health and economic prospects. They take advantage of digital tools to analyze issues that interest them and navigate online resources to guide their own learning. If they have questions that extend beyond their teachers' expertise, they track down outside experts to help them figure out what they want to learn. They get their own work into the world, too, by publishing on online platforms and making convincing pitches to public audiences and government councils. It's hard not to feel hopeful after talking to students engaged in these kinds of authentic learning experiences.

While attending a global youth conference in Shanghai, I sat down with student delegates from Northwest Passage High School, a project-based school in Coon Rapids, Minnesota (Boss, 2014b). The conference challenged them to work in small teams with Chinese and U.S. peers they had just met and devise solutions to compelling global issues related to health, education, and the environment. The students with PBL experience thrived, in many cases taking leadership roles on their teams. "We're used to collaborating, figuring out how to define problems, and identifying our audience," they told me. Students from more traditional schools, they noticed, struggled "without a lot of instruction. . . . We understand what it means to take control of our own education."

Changing Roles

Students who have regular opportunities to take part in engaging, academically challenging PBL are still outliers in the education landscape, but their ranks are growing. Motivated by a desire to better prepare students for the challenges of college, careers, and citizenship, increasing numbers of teachers, school networks, and entire school systems are making a shift to project-based learning enabled by digital tools.

If you are considering this shift—for your classroom or an entire school system—recognize from the outset that it may not be easy.

PBL demands new roles for teachers and students alike. In *Reinventing Project-Based Learning*, coauthor Jane Krauss and I (2014) document several changes that teachers can anticipate, including the following.

- **Learning goals:** Reconsider what you expect students to know and do.

- **Ways of talking and engaging with students:** Interact with your students in different ways. Get comfortable with *messier learning*, with students working more autonomously (and not necessarily all doing the same thing at the same time).

- **Classroom management style:** Help students better handle their own growth.

- **Physical classroom arrangement:** Reposition the classroom fixtures to enable teamwork and collaboration.

- **Assessment thinking:** Re-evaluate what you take note of during the learning process and adjust your teaching plan based on what you notice.

- **Collected materials:** Reconsider which learning artifacts you preserve.

- **Communication with parents and colleagues:** Defend the thinking behind the 21st century project approach, and encourage parents and other community members to find ways to support project work. For example, they might provide audience feedback, share their expertise, or help with the logistics of field research.

Teachers become change agents through these shifts, turning theories about education reform into noticeable differences in day-to-day learning experiences. School change experts Michael Fullan and Donnelly (2013) describe such reinvented classrooms in *Alive in the Swamp*: "Problems and questions are placed in real world contexts; the emphasis is on intellectual risk taking and trial-and-error problem solving; and there is a healthy partnership between the student and teacher that is built on enquiry and data" (p. 16).

Fortunately, teachers don't have to figure out all these changes on their own. Educators who have already traveled this path provide insights for their colleagues to borrow and adapt. Rich examples help newcomers make a faster transition to teaching with real-world projects, answering Fullan and Langworthy's (2013) call for more models that show "what teaching for this kind of connected and flourishing learning looks like" (p. 11).

Learning From Pioneers

In the vanguard of this nascent PBL movement are networks of schools that deliver all their instruction through projects. To leverage their collective wisdom, these PBL pioneers—including High Tech High, the New Tech Network, Expeditionary Learning, Envision Learning, and others—have joined the Deeper Learning Network, an initiative of the William and Flora Hewlett Foundation. By coming together as a network, they are in a better position to collaborate, share and model best practices, and communicate with the larger education field about how to achieve lasting school change (Boss & Krauss, 2014).

Although their models vary somewhat, they typically emphasize student-driven inquiry, authentic problem solving, and access to technology. Teachers in these settings rise to the challenge of being curriculum designers. They leverage peer collaboration, critiquing, and, often, instructional coaching to improve their practice.

Schools at the forefront of this movement tend to be transparent about their systemic approaches to rethinking education through PBL. They open their classrooms to visitors and, in many cases, make project examples and resources publicly available. That's good news for educators who want to see PBL in action before taking the plunge themselves.

The Buck Institute for Education, a nonprofit that focuses on improving education globally, has been another driver of change, helping teachers and school systems around the world design and implement high-quality PBL. (Visit the Buck Institute for Education website [http://bie.org] for downloadable PBL planning resources. Full disclosure: I'm part of the Buck Institute for Education faculty and have collaborated on publications.)

Stand-alone schools, such as the well-respected Science Leadership Academy in Philadelphia, Pennsylvania, also share their PBL success stories and instructional strategies. The Science Leadership Academy hosts an annual conference, EduCon, that attracts hundreds of educators to its urban campus for conversations about reimagining K–12 education. Students at Science Leadership Academy take part in these conversations, reflecting on the projects that have challenged and inspired them, such as following in Alexis de Tocqueville's footsteps to become modern-day historians themselves, using their understanding of science to design a solar-powered water purifier for the developing world, or teaching lessons about social justice and civil rights to middle schoolers in their community.

These pioneering schools' strong results, along with mounting evidence about the effectiveness of PBL, have sparked interest in project-based learning in more mainstream settings. Since the 1990s, researchers have documented a range of benefits for PBL, including increased motivation and engagement, deeper understanding of academic content, and enhanced problem-solving skills (Finkelstein, Hanson, Huang, Hirschman, & Huang, 2010; Mergendoller, Maxwell, & Bellisimo, 2006; Stites, 1998; Thomas, 2000). A 2014 study of schools in the Deeper Learning Network, which includes the PBL schools mentioned previously, reports higher graduation rates, better test scores, and stronger interpersonal skills compared to more traditional schools (Zeiser, Taylor, Rickles, Garet, & Segeritz, 2014).

Bob Lenz, cofounder of Envision Education and incoming executive director of the Buck Institute for Education, finds particularly hopeful news embedded in this research. Blogging about the Deeper Learning Network research, he comments on the evidence of equity in PBL settings:

> Perhaps two of the most significant findings from the list [of outcomes] above are that students are developing higher levels of academic engagement, collaboration, motivation, and self efficacy and that deeper learning is working with students regardless of their income levels or prior school achievement . . . Deeper learning strategies are giving *all kids* the opportunities, experiences, and skills each of us want for our own children. (Lenz, 2014)

Given the inequities that persist in education, this is hopeful news, indeed. Students who will be the first in their families to attend college dominate the California schools in the Envision network. (For a more comprehensive look at the research on PBL, see Vega, 2012, and visit **go.solution-tree.com/technology** to access the link.)

As PBL spreads from early-adopter schools to more mainstream contexts, various implementation models emerge. A shift to PBL sometimes starts at the grass roots with a core group of teachers who become advance scouts for their colleagues. Or an entire faculty or professional learning community might participate in professional development together to learn PBL fundamentals. In many schools, technology rollouts are the precipitating factors for rethinking instruction that leverages digital tools in new ways.

Instead of doing all projects all the time, some schools have students engage in PBL only a few times a year or just in certain disciplines, such as science, technology, engineering, and mathematics (STEM) or career and technical education. Even in smaller doses, PBL can produce transformative results if it helps students recognize their potential and see how school relates to their interests.

Whether projects last for a couple of weeks or an entire semester and whether they focus on one content area or cross disciplines, the same strategies apply. To make the most of the learning opportunities that PBL affords, keep in mind the following four core ideas (Boss & Krauss, 2014).

1. The inquiry project, framed by a driving question, is the centerpiece of instruction. It's not an add-on or hands-on activity wrapping up a unit of study. Instead, the project is designed with specific learning goals in mind.

2. Students get involved in real-world problem solving, applying the strategies and tools used in authentic disciplines and, often, engaging with outside experts.

3. Students share their work with authentic audiences.

4. Technology is used as a means for students to collaborate, communicate, and make discoveries they wouldn't otherwise gain.

By giving students a reason to engage and the opportunity to discover their passions and talents, PBL may help address the worrisome decline in student optimism discussed previously. Connie Rath, vice chair of Gallup Education, highlights this glimmer of positive news in a six-hundred-thousand-student Gallup survey:

> Students who strongly agreed that their school is committed to building students' strengths *and* that they have a teacher who makes them excited about the future are almost 30 times as likely to be engaged learners as their peers who strongly disagreed with both statements. (Gallup, 2014, p. 3)

About This Book

Implementing Project-Based Learning draws on the four core ideas, using my own experience with schools implementing PBL and interviews with teachers and students, to set the stage for rigorous, relevant, digital-age learning that excites students about the future.

Teachers who were the designers of the creative projects you will read about in the coming pages reflected on their PBL experiences in post-project interviews. Unless otherwise indicated, interviews took place during December 2014.

Chapter 1 lays the foundation for PBL, identifying the environment and critical skills essential to success and four phases every well-designed project goes through. Then, in chapters 2 through 6, I delve into five specific types of PBL: (1) geoliteracy projects, (2) data literacy projects, (3) entrepreneurship and innovation projects, (4) media literacy projects, and (5) storytelling projects. In the examples in chapters 2 through 6, you will read about projects that deliberately build on students' strengths while introducing them to new ways of thinking and problem solving. Each chapter ends with helpful resources to get started with PBL. Finally, in chapter 7, I outline some challenges teachers face and questions they have when implementing PBL and offer assessment strategies. Visit **go.solution-tree .com/technology** to access materials related to this book.

As teachers reflect on successful project experiences, you can sense the contagious excitement that they bring into the classroom. The stories in the following chapters exemplify the reconsidered school experiences that "blow the lid off learning, whereby students and teachers as partners become captivated by education" (Fullan & Langworthy, 2013, p. 1). Can you picture your students in similar roles, learning by engaging with real issues and then sharing their project results with an appreciative audience? When students produce work that is taken seriously, that solves genuine problems, and that matters to them and the larger world, all of us have cause to be more optimistic about the future. So, let's get started.

Chapter 1

A Strong Foundation—and Then Some

In *Leading the New Literacies*, curriculum expert Heidi Hayes Jacobs (2014) describes 21st century educators as standing at a busy crossroads. Buffeted by rapid change and quickly evolving forms of communication, teachers and school leaders must confront decisions about how to cultivate literate learners in these new arenas. Standing still is not an option if we want students to master the literacies and tools they need to fully engage with their 21st century world.

Consider your current learning environment. Is it a destination where students make meaning with the use of digital tools and ready access to information? Do they take that information at face value, or do they evaluate source material for reliability or bias? Is the curriculum prescribed with predictable outcomes, or is it flexible enough for students to explore interests and discover what matters to them? Do they have opportunities to be makers and content creators themselves, sharing their work with authentic audiences? Does learning stop at the classroom door or extend into the wider world through connected learning experiences that develop students' global competency?

The New Literacies

An environment that's been reimagined to better engage 21st century learners expands our traditional understanding of literacy. Jacobs (2014) classifies new literacies into three broad categories: (1) digital, (2) media, and (3) global. Rather than calling for a wholesale replacement of traditional education, however, she suggests looking for intersections and fusions of old and new approaches to learning.

In project-based learning, it's not unusual to combine digital literacy, media production, and global connections in the course of answering a driving question. This may sound daunting if you're a newcomer to PBL, but we can learn from observing teachers—and students—who have made the journey to digital-age projects. Some deliberately cultivate the literacies that Jacobs (2014) describes. Others push into even newer territory, leveraging cutting-edge tools and introducing students to specialized strategies for problem solving.

Even the most innovative project examples build on a familiar foundation. PBL doesn't require us to discard teaching and learning strategies that we know work well. For example, the essential skills of reading, writing, listening, and speaking all come into play in PBL, regardless of project focus. From the earliest elementary years to the most advanced high school courses, students engage in projects through questioning, researching, close reading, analyzing, and, often, multimedia writing and publishing.

Whether students engage with resources that their teacher has curated or they search for their own source material, they need to evaluate what they read for reliability. When students collaborate with peers, consult with content-area experts, or make public presentations of their findings, they use communication skills. Across curricula, these familiar skills are indispensable in PBL. PBL teachers don't consider these important skills to be too *old school* for 21st century students. Instead, they look for opportunities to reinforce them in projects that connect with students' interests.

Teachers can support students' project success by incorporating learning activities that build a strong foundation of literacy and critical thinking. For example, writers' workshops and close-reading techniques may prove useful not only in language arts but also in projects that address social studies or science standards. The same goes for protocols for active class discussions (such as the Socratic seminar and Harkness table methods). Discussions will be more productive if teachers deliberately teach and model how to elaborate, disagree, and make counterarguments. In projects that focus on mathematics and science standards, students use literacy skills for an authentic purpose when they communicate their results with a public audience. All these skills—new and old—are invaluable in building the foundation for PBL.

Four Phases of PBL

The Buck Institute for Education (Boss, 2013) has identified four phases that happen in every well-designed project.

1. **Project launch:** This typically starts with an entry event to ignite curiosity and introduces a driving question to frame the inquiry experience.

2. **Knowledge building:** Students build background understanding and learn new skills to help them answer the driving question.

3. **Product development and critique:** Students apply what they have learned to create something new (such as a product, solution, or recommendation).

4. **Final presentation and reflection:** Students share their polished work with an authentic audience.

All along this pathway, teachers can scaffold the learning experience by anticipating and responding to diverse learners' needs and customizing instruction accordingly. Some students, for example, may need deliberate instruction and modeling to learn how to collaborate or provide peer critique effectively. Students working on the same project may bring different background knowledge and have diverse academic strengths. During a project, teachers might offer mini-lessons for students who need specific instruction or support, leaving others to work independently or with their team members. The project framework is loose enough to allow for personalization and differentiation yet tight enough to ensure that learning goals are addressed for all. Some projects go well beyond the basics to encourage specialized ways of thinking and problem solving that are useful both in school and in life beyond the classroom.

In the examples in the following chapters, we'll take a close look at an expanded set of digital-age literacies and the kinds of projects that help students acquire them. You'll hear about projects that challenge students to make sense of data, craft compelling stories, and bring visual thinking into problem solving. Other projects build students' media literacy skills and put students on the path to active citizenship, either globally or locally.

In many of the examples, you'll see students taking advantage of emerging technological tools and platforms. That's in keeping with Fullan and Donnelly's (2013) advice that technology should be "irresistibly engaging for the learner. . . . In the best innovations, digital tools are participatory, engaging, co-creative, and collaborative" (p. 21).

At the same time, you'll notice that technology itself is not the primary project focus; it's simply another tool to help students achieve ambitious learning goals. "This is not about the technology," insists Robert Kolvoord, founder of the Geospatial Semester program and pioneering educator who regularly introduces students and teachers to geographic information system (GIS) software for problem solving. "When some people see this complicated software, it's full stop for them. These projects are about students and teachers investigating interesting things and solving problems together. Technology is simply a vehicle."

Some of the examples ahead connect to trends taking hold outside the classroom. The *big data* movement, crowdsourcing of information, and the push for innovation across diverse sectors are among the developments that will likely affect how students interact with their world in the near future. Introductions to these trends may turn into career pathways for some 21st century students, and projects often create opportunities to learn from professionals in these emerging fields. Even projects that are on the cutting edge are scaled to the right size and complexity for student understanding.

When digital learners rise to the challenge of real-world problem solving, they acquire a set of skills that will serve them well, long after they leave the classroom (Gallup, 2014). According to media literacy teacher Chris Sperry (2012), "In the 21st century, these are no longer 'elective' skills" (p. 49).

Chapter 2
Geoliteracy Projects: Making Global Connections

When Mike Wagner piloted a new course called Geospatial Semester at Heritage High School in Leesburg, Virginia, during the 2006 to 2007 school year, he remembers feeling "completely out of my comfort zone." Although he was a veteran science teacher, he was largely unfamiliar with geographic information system software, which allows users to visualize and analyze data by creating layered maps. Students were a bit perplexed, too, when their teacher asked them to come up with their own ideas for projects about local issues that they might investigate. "A lot of them struggled at first with learning to think critically and ask good questions," he recalls. "They hadn't had much experience with that in the earlier grades."

Nearly a decade later, Wagner and his students have become adept at collecting, analyzing, and presenting geographic data to address real issues in their community. Where is the best location for offshore wind farms to maximize efficiency and minimize unsightliness? How might a terror threat affect local roads and public services? These are among the issues that his students have explored and explained for public audiences through geospatial projects.

"It all starts with getting students to think critically about the data that they're seeing," Wagner explains. Mapping tools are helpful, but they are not the main focus of these projects. "This is about connecting students to their place in the world," Wagner says.

Learning to organize, visualize, and analyze information that relates to global and local issues is critical preparation for living in our connected and fast-changing world. Concerned about a lack of resources for what it calls *geo-education*, the National Geographic Society is part of a new coalition to bring greater attention to the need for this kind of thinking.

According to Daniel Edelson (2013), formerly vice president for education at the National Geographic Society and executive director of the National Geographic Education Foundation, geo-education prepares us to make choices about how to interact with others in our complex world. He argues that geo-education also prepares us to make decisions in our professional lives about resources and systems. Teaching students to understand the interconnectedness of systems will get them ready to deal with civic challenges—whether that means "globalization, military conflicts, community development, environmental threats, depletion of natural resources," or other issues yet to unfold (Edelson, 2013).

"To overgeneralize, location matters," says Robert Kolvoord. "That's the geographer's point of view. The geographer is particularly interested in *why* things are where they are."

The spatial thinking that happens when students make and analyze maps, Kolvoord adds, "is useful for students who want to go into STEM careers. The geographic focus is useful for anybody who wants to be an informed citizen. An awful lot of data are presented to us in the form of maps. As citizens, we need to make decisions and be informed based on those kinds of presentations. We spend far too little time doing that, particularly in K–12 schools."

A similar message comes from Stewart Kirkpatrick, GIS coordinator for the state of Montana. Government agencies "are doing much more with crowdsourced data. We have limited staff. We can put out open street maps, for example, and people can add information to correct boundaries or addresses. This gets citizens involved [in government]." Being able to work with geospatial information is a skill of the future, he predicts. "When today's K–12 students get into college, they're going to be expected to be able to collect data, process data, display data," he says, whether their studies focus on biology or business.

Kolvoord designed the Geospatial Semester program, now offered in high schools across Virginia, to solve a worrisome problem. "We saw students coming out of high school not ready to do college-level work. They're just as capable as students of a generation ago," he's quick to add, "but they were not coming ready to do what they needed to be able to do." He blames a decade of high-stakes testing, and the test-prep curriculum that goes along with it, for hampering the development of key competencies such as critical thinking and problem solving.

The Geospatial Semester is specifically designed for the end of high school—lost time, academically, for many seniors. Kolvoord envisioned his course offering seniors "opportunities at the tail end of high school that could serve as a transition into college, work, or the armed forces. It would allow them to learn marketable skills and deal with real-world problems."

Although the project attracts some students because of the chance to use professional-grade digital tools, Kolvoord downplays the technology angle when he talks about the program with interested school districts: "Some people focus on the fact that ArcView [GIS mapping software] is a powerful piece of software. That can get in the way of thinking about what kids can do with it."

Many students come to geospatial projects with little background in geography. "That's not a focus of the middle school or high school curriculum. As a consequence, students may see maps regularly, but they aren't thinking about the content of those maps or what went into making them," Kolvoord says. "They're not often forced to do much interpretation. We ask them to take what's in front of them and think about what's behind it."

To help students develop geospatial thinking, teachers can "ask students to think critically when they look at maps and to think about things like proximity or clustering in space. Where are things located in relation to other things? Then," Kolvoord adds, "you can encourage them to use that information as a way to reason." Looking at maps that show the populations of different ethnic groups in the United States, for example, can provide an opportunity to ask students, "Why did this distribution come about? How have patterns changed over time? What are the trends to expect as we look to the future?"

These conversations can happen outside of PBL, of course, but when projects incorporate geoliteracy as part of authentic problem solving, the results can be valuable for students and communities alike. "Students pick a problem that's interesting to them and then explore it," Kolvoord explains. That invitation to select a topic sparks engagement. "Students have very little choice in high school," he adds. "When given the opportunity to do something of interest, they grab on and are willing to grapple with it."

Kolvoord has seen students explore local Wi-Fi coverage and food deserts in their communities, investigate pollution prevalence in rural areas, and recommend the best location for a new NFL franchise. One girl from a dairy farming family decided to trace the *milkshed* of the region where her family farm is located. She discovered that much of the milk from the local herd wound up being dehydrated and exported overseas as milk powder. The project helped her understand and explain global supply chains in agribusiness.

One of the challenges students encounter in PBL, Kolvoord says, "is not only finding a problem worth solving but finding a problem that's solvable. They have to consider the time that they have and the data that are available. Part of the problem-solving process is figuring out what the constraints are. That's where we push students on the critical-thinking front."

In PBL, as noted in chapter 1, a defining characteristic of projects is a culminating public presentation or demonstration of results. In Geospatial Semester projects at James Madison University, students make final presentations to a panel of college faculty. "Students have to stand up, present their work, and get poked and prodded a bit. This helps them anticipate what's coming [in college and careers]. They're moving out of a place where there's always a right answer to a time when there may not be a right answer. They learn that there are better-argued answers and better-supported answers. This isn't easy for many students," Kolvoord acknowledges.

Teacher Mike Wagner acknowledges that some students "struggle to communicate their data in a visual way. The biggest challenge isn't getting the data or analyzing it but figuring out how to communicate it." Presenting complex information in a visually interesting way is an increasingly valued skill in fields ranging from science to business to new media. Students working on GIS projects know they have succeeded when they can "put their map on a wall and everybody who reads it can understand it," Wagner adds. That's authentic feedback.

There's no need for students to wait until high school to start developing geospatial thinking. To show elementary teachers the possibilities of geospatial thinking, Wagner might share a story map about migration made to accompany a children's book called *Bird, Butterfly, Eel* (Prosek, 2009). He says, "The story map takes the information in the book and makes it visual. Students can talk about, 'Where would we go in our county to see a barn swallow?' There's a difference between just reading a book about migration and seeing it visually on a map that lets you zoom in and out."

Virginia is one of a handful of states where students develop geospatial thinking skills in the course of addressing community issues. Similar projects happen regularly in schools that are part of the multistate Environmental and Spatial Technology (EAST) Initiative based in Arkansas. EAST students engage in PBL that incorporates technology and delivers community service. In past projects, EAST students have plotted the best evacuation routes in case of natural disaster, created multimedia story maps to document local history, and mapped national park trails.

"There's a common element across the curriculum, and it's place," says Montana GIS coordinator Stewart Kirkpatrick. "Geography is the glue that can connect all subject areas."

In Montana, students have used GIS tools to map everything from water mains to manhole covers to bat habitats. Visitors to a small-town cemetery dating back to pioneer days can now locate the grave sites of their ancestors, thanks to accurate maps created by high school students.

Gail Shatkus, GIS coordinator for Chester-Joplin-Inverness Schools in Montana and assistant professor at Montana State University-Northern, says one of these projects' greatest values has little to do with geospatial thinking. "It's having students work with adults in the community. Students become on a par [with adults] when they have to ask for information or explain their results," she says. With mentoring, students "become comfortable talking in front of the county commission. They become confident about calling a state engineer. They can go out and find solutions themselves. That's what we're really looking for—that initiative. It's going to help them in whatever they choose to do next," says Shatkus.

Many projects involve community partners. Kolvoord says, "Students are empowered by the fact that adults take their work seriously. Their work is validated. In those interactions, students also start to see how professionals work and think. That's what we hope for in all our interactions with industry."

Shatkus also appreciates "that it's not just me encouraging the students. It's the local community, local surveyors, county commissioners." She and other adult experts once accompanied a group of students to a nearby mountaintop to see if they could detect a GPS signal. "We got on four-wheelers and went up the mountain. Students got a centimeter-accurate reading at the top. Best of all, it was their project. The adults didn't touch the equipment. The kids did it all."

How to Get Started With Geoliteracy Projects

Geoliteracy projects can involve a wide range of content areas and grade levels. What connects these learning experiences is a focus on place.

Consider projects that get students thinking critically about why artifacts, landmarks, people, or wildlife are located where they are. Driving questions might ask, "How can we create a visitor map of public art (or historic landmarks, wildlife viewing sites, or unique attractions) in our community? How can we prevent bike accidents at the most dangerous intersections in town? Where should the city add sidewalks to encourage walking for exercise?" A project with a historical focus might have students making before-and-after comparisons of important events and places.

To help troubleshoot technology challenges with geospatial projects, Gail Shatkus recommends recruiting a core team of students to become resident GIS experts. Her high school students plan learning activities appropriate for different grade levels and coach teachers on technology use. "You've heard of *flipping the classroom*? I call this *flipping the teacher*," she says.

More resources and inspiration for geoliteracy projects are available on the following websites.

- Esri EdCommunity (http://edcommunity.esri.com) is a source for GIS resources and teacher-created GIS lessons.

- Promise of Place (http://promiseofplace.org) offers resources and research about place-based education.

- Story Maps (http://storymaps.arcgis.com/en) enable users to combine maps with multimedia content about literature or nonfiction research.

- Google Lit Trips (http://googlelittrips.com) is a teacher- and student-developed resource that turns works of great literature into interactive maps. As characters in *The Grapes of Wrath* (Steinbeck, 1939) make their epic Dust Bowl journey, for example, readers can explore the media embedded in an accompanying Lit Trip map. Some students are motivated to make their own Google Lit Trips about the books that move them.

- The Environmental and Spatial Technology Initiative maintains a project finder (http://eastinitiative.org /projectsschools/projectfinder.aspx) to share highlights of projects that combine PBL with service learning, often with a geospatial focus.

Chapter 3

Data Literacy Projects: Understanding Big Data

We live in a world awash in data. Every Google search, ad click-through, standardized test, public health report, and political poll adds to the mountains of information available for analysis.

From the World Bank to local government bureaus, organizations are becoming increasingly transparent about the information that they gather. People who know how to analyze and interpret open data can crunch numbers to make predictions, explain historical trends, or poke holes in faulty arguments. Increasingly, data scientists leverage their specialized insights to address social and environmental challenges, from climate change to global poverty. Some cities have improved local services by inviting citizens to crowdsource data about needed park repairs or potholes in need of filling.

Students who become data literate enjoy an advantage when it comes to problem solving. They get a head start on posing good questions, analyzing information, and supporting their conclusions with reliable evidence. "Analyzing data, spotting patterns, and extracting useful information have become gateway skills to full participation in the workforce and civic engagement of the 21st century," according to the Oceans of Data Institute, an initiative of the Learning and Teaching Division at the Education Development Center (EDC Oceans of Data Institute, n.d.b).

Yet few students have had occasion to do much data analysis in the K–12 years (unless they take a statistics class). That's starting to change, thanks in part to new projects and platforms that enable students to explore issues through data analysis.

Tuva Labs (https://tuvalabs.com) is a good example (Boss, 2014a). This educational platform connects students and teachers with open data sets and analytical tools to help them make sense of their world. The idea for Tuva Labs emerged when cofounder Harshil Parikh was tutoring children in the slums of Delhi, India. "I was looking for tools to drive inquiry," he recalls.

Parikh knows through his experience as an engineer, an educator, and a social entrepreneur that curiosity is a powerful motivator for learning. However, learning won't happen with curiosity alone. Students need to investigate and use critical thinking to arrive at answers they can trust. Enter Tuva Labs. When students (or teachers) post questions on the site, Parikh and his team get busy scouring sources of publicly available data that relate to the topic. Students then use data to investigate a range of questions: How does my high school compare to others in the United States when it comes to SAT scores? How can we use statistics to measure global happiness? How have different military branches changed in size over time? Tuva Labs curates data sets to make the information more accessible to students and teachers. That curated information might include "context about an issue, offer background about the data source, or suggest specific strategies to represent information visually. We want to be a bridge between schools and the open data movement," Parikh explains.

He's also eager to encourage teachers to look beyond mathematics class when they think about projects that might include data analysis. That means social studies or English teachers may need to brush up on their own data skills or look for opportunities to collaborate with colleagues who have expertise.

Eleanor Terry, who teaches high school mathematics and statistics, says she's the go-to person at her school for any teacher looking to incorporate data analysis into a project (Boss, 2014a). In her own classroom, she uses open data to give students more voice and choice as they learn mathematics concepts. "We might all be working on scatterplots or standard deviation, but students can choose which data set to use," she explains. While some students may be drawn to sports, other students might want to focus on a social justice matter, like human trafficking. "They're all learning the same math concepts, but with more student choice. That's not always easy to do in math," she adds. Students are more likely to ask searching questions when they pick the topics they survey. "If they get to choose a data set that interests them, then I can ask, 'What do you want to know about that?' It's a much better entry point for thinking about statistics," she says.

The Census at School project offers another example. This international project for students in grades 4–12 began in the United Kingdom and has expanded to the United States with support from the American Statistical Association. "Students complete an online survey, analyze their class census results, and compare their class with random samples of students in the United States and other participating countries" (American Statistical Association, 2010, p. 4). Students then engage in statistical problem solving by formulating new questions that the data can help answer (American Statistical Association, 2010).

There's also a civic education aspect to this project. The students investigate questions such as, "How does a government go about collecting information from its citizens? How do we reach every American? What can the census tell us about changing demographics and about our own perceptions? These are powerful ideas," says Parikh. These ideas can connect data analysis to social studies and other disciplines. If students start with survey information about themselves and their peers, he adds, "that's as authentic as it gets. Students need opportunities to get their hands dirty with data."

Another example challenged students to use data analysis to think about a hard-to-measure quality: happiness. Designed by the New Tech Network and hosted on Tuva Labs, the Global Happiness Project, which took place in 2014, involved students from some two hundred classrooms, elementary through high school, in surveys about what makes people happy. Each class took its own approach to answering the driving question, "How can we use data, creativity, and community to make the world a happier place?" (New Tech Network, 2014). A health teacher worked with junior high students to improve the happiness level at their school by promoting healthy behaviors and discouraging bullying. Meanwhile, a high school language arts teacher integrated data analysis about happiness into literature studies. Students analyzed how different novelists and nonfiction writers interpret happiness, and then they applied their own creativity to service projects that made their community a happier place.

In the wake of high-profile news events—such as the police shooting in Ferguson, Missouri, or the choke-hold death of an African American man in Staten Island, New York—many teachers are looking for projects that address social justice themes. Starting with data analysis "is an ideal way for students to dig into an [emotionally charged] issue," Parikh says. "Teachers are realizing they need to give students opportunities to question the things they're presented with, whether it's a news article or story unfolding in their community or internationally. What do the data say?"

The Ebola outbreak in 2014 provided students with another real-life example of the usefulness of modeling and prediction. Parikh says, "Conversations about how fast the virus was spreading or how long it takes for symptoms to surface came down to asking, 'What do the data say?' Teachers and students could see the value of good data collection, modeling, and making predictions."

How to Get Started With Data Literacy Projects

Encourage data literacy from an early age by asking students to think carefully about the statistics and predictions they encounter, everywhere from the world of sports and entertainment to politics and popular science. Are the numbers reliable? Are they surprising? Why? What can students find out about the source of information?

In a project that involves polling or other forms of data gathering, challenge students to analyze their results and tell a story with their data. As they prepare for public presentations, remind them to consider, "What's the best way to present this information visually? How can I make my data understandable and interesting to others?"

The following digital tools can help students make infographics, or visual representations of data.

- Lucidchart (www.lucidchart.com) can be used to draw flowcharts, mind maps, and other graphics.

- Many Eyes (www-969.ibm.com/software/analytics /manyeyes) is a free platform for creating and sharing visualizations in various formats, from word clouds to bubble charts.

- The *New York Times*, itself a good source of infographics, offers a collection of infographics resources for educators. Start with the blog post "Teaching With Infographics: Places to Start" (Schulten, 2010).

More resources for incorporating data literacy into PBL (in addition to Tuva Labs) include the following outlets.

- Census at School (www.amstat.org/censusatschool /index.cfm) is an educational project of the American Statistical Association.

- SurveyMonkey (www.surveymonkey.com) and Google Forms (www.google.com/forms/about) are among the options for creating online surveys.

- The Common Online Data Analysis Platform (CODAP; http://concord.org/projects/codap) is a project from the Concord Consortium that offers dynamic technology tools to engage with data.

Chapter 4

Entrepreneurship and Innovation Projects: Understanding the Business World

The thought of spending your life in the same career—let alone working for the same employer—sounds nostalgic, at best, to today's young people. And no wonder. Rapid shifts in the world economy demand flexible, adaptable thinkers who have a global perspective. Many 21st century learners may wind up working in fields not yet imagined, using technologies not yet invented.

Projects that emphasize entrepreneurship and innovation put students on a fast track to becoming tomorrow's opportunity creators. Knowing how to solve problems creatively and convince others of the value of your ideas are skills that matter across a wide range of fields—from STEM to self-employment to social entrepreneurship. The Network for Teaching Entrepreneurship (n.d.), which focuses on developing these capabilities in low-income youth, argues that entrepreneurship education offers a "fundamental tool for creating an ongoing cycle of learning and innovation."

Global education expert Yong Zhao (2014) explains why entrepreneurship has become an essential skill in a world where youth unemployment is rampant. "Entrepreneur-oriented education prepares children to take the responsibility of creating jobs," he explains (p. 184). That's a contrast to "employee-oriented education," which prepares students to fit existing (and quickly diminishing) work opportunities. "As traditional routine jobs are offshored and automated, we need more and more globally competent, creative, innovative, entrepreneurship-minded citizens who are job creators instead of employment-minded job seekers" (Zhao, 2014, p. 189).

Two projects—(1) Shark Tank and (2) Vog Scrubber—illustrate the wide range of possibilities for student innovators. As you read about these examples, watch for evidence of the entrepreneur-oriented skills that Zhao (2014) endorses: variation, diversity, tolerance, autonomy, passion, and interest.

Shark Tank

Shark Tank, a popular reality TV show in which aspiring entrepreneurs pitch to investors, got a makeover in this classroom project involving aquaponics.

Raleigh Werberger, originally a history and humanities teacher, found his way to teaching entrepreneurship out of a desire to revive his students' intrinsic motivation to learn. He recognized that a prescribed curriculum wasn't engaging all learners. "Some students just want to get a good score to get into college, but that's really about pleasing the teacher. I wanted to make the work more intrinsically rewarding," he says. "How could I create space to let kids dive into things so they can go more deeply, and also the space for them to find their own interests?"

Answers emerged in 2013 when he teamed up with a colleague to design a PBL-based program for ninth graders at Mid-Pacific Institute in Manoa, Hawaii. "We wanted a project that would encompass the whole year. So we did reverse engineering: we started with the project idea and wrapped the curriculum into it," Werberger says. As an engaging focus to connect disciplines, they chose sustainability, a real-world topic with high student interest. Werberger and his teaching partner also were influenced by reading Yong Zhao's (2012) *World Class Learners*, which makes a case for students producing work of real value.

To help students focus on creating a useful, sustainable product, they narrowed the focus to aquaponics. This sustainable system for raising plants and fish has connections to local Hawaiian culture and offers opportunities for small-business start-ups. Through more teacher collaboration, a driving question emerged to frame the extended, in-depth inquiry: How can we design and market an aquaponics kit for the home?

On the STEM side of the project, students studied systems and ecology. They visited local aquaponics farms to learn about sustainable agribusiness and produced infographics to explain how closed systems work. NASA's (2013) engineering and design process helped them brainstorm ideas and design their own aquaponics kits. They learned how to give and receive peer critique to improve their designs, working with sketches and cardboard models before building prototypes with Plexiglas and more permanent materials.

Meanwhile, Werberger had no trouble incorporating language arts content into the project. Students read the biography of Steve Jobs (Isaacson, 2011) to analyze how innovators think. They deconstructed everything from dystopian fiction to crowdfunding campaigns on Kickstarter (www.kickstarter.com), looking for examples of effective persuasion and rhetorical devices. In a blog post about the project, Werberger (2014) reflects:

> Understanding narrative began to matter more as students realized they had to craft a compelling message for their campaigns. As they learned the importance of communication in the professional world, writing

exercises became a common-sense preparation for
life, not a chore. My STEM partners reported the same
results for math and science lessons. In other words,
the students saw the adoption of classroom skills as
an important step for their future success.

As the teacher introduced new topics, he noticed, "I had [stu-
dent] buy-in for almost anything I did. Every time we went to a
new subject, it was easy for me to ask, 'OK, why are we doing this?'
Kids would say, 'It's because we have to learn _____ for
the project.' There was a purposefulness that was lacking in other
courses."

To manage the project, teams were organized around specific roles
that students chose for themselves. "Some kids are really good at
building. They self-selected the engineer role. Others are more interested in the design aspects. They drew the blueprints." Students who
gravitate to writing worked on the marketing campaign, while those
with talents in conflict resolution and leadership took on the role of
contractor. "The contractor's job was to make sure everybody was
doing what they needed to do and to be the point of contact for
each team [with the teachers]," Werberger explains.

The ambitious project generated considerable buzz in the community. Parents who heard about the project around the kitchen
table offered their insights. If students needed more technical help
or troubleshooting, they used social media to spread the word and
enlist specific expertise. Volunteers emerged from a local makerspace
(a community workshop equipped with tools for prototyping), a
business incubator, and an aquaponics hobbyist group.

Werberger recalls one particularly busy day near the end of the
project: "We had two investors in class to run a business boot camp.
Parents who are contractors were consulting with some students.
Reporters from the *Honolulu Star-Advertiser* were doing interviews.
That's when the principal came in. He had seen this train of adults

coming in to work with our students. It was inspirational, just watching. The energy and excitement in the room were palpable."

The project concluded with a *Shark Tank*–style pitch session, held in the community makerspace. Teams vied for $1,500 in real funding from local investors, putting their rhetorical skills to effective use. "Even the shy students stood up in front of this massive crowd and made their presentations," Werberger says. He recalls the event as "a great community-building moment," with value going beyond any financial rewards. "This was about doing something authentic. This project told students, 'Your work has value.'"

Vog Scrubber

By coincidence, a second PBL example that emphasizes entrepreneurship and innovation also comes from Hawaii. In this case, it's about students responding to an unusual local situation: living in the shadow of an active volcano.

Eric Clause is the STEM coordinator at the Hawai'i Academy of Arts and Science, a public charter school in Pāhoa, Hawaii. Clause came to teaching as a second career and brings private-sector experience in science and engineering. He teaches about 120 students in grades 7–12.

Clause didn't have to search far to find a STEM problem for his students to tackle. In fact, they identified it themselves. In 2014, lava flows from the nearby Kilauea volcano were approaching their small community. When Clause asked students about possible ill effects from the lava flow, one student responded, "The vog, obviously!" *Vog* is volcanic fog, a gaseous discharge that smells like rotten eggs and can pose dangers to people with asthma and other respiratory conditions. Air conditioners and air filters aren't designed to eliminate what's in vog. With this authentic problem affecting their own families and classmates, students wondered if they could leverage their understanding of STEM to invent an inexpensive device that would clean vog from the air.

Although the project eventually got into marketing and entrepreneurial concepts, that's not where it started. "My students wanted to do something to help our community. That was their initial inspiration for the project," Clause recalls. "It's a student-driven project that grew out of a real need."

Tackling the project gave Clause a chance to guide students through lessons in both chemistry and engineering. They learned that vog is composed of extremely acidic compounds that bond with moisture in the air. "When it reaches the lungs, it's sulfuric acid—same as you'd find in a car battery," the teacher explains. Laboratory experiments gave them opportunities to try to neutralize the acid, learning through experience about balancing chemical equations.

Using ready-made materials they could find in a hardware store—an innovation strategy for rapid engineering—students designed a *vog scrubber*. It pushes a column of acidic air down to a vat of water that's been mixed with a base (in this case, a compound similar to baking soda) to neutralize the acid. "What you get is salt that settles to the bottom and clean air." In effect, students repurposed that old science fair standby—the vinegar and baking soda volcano—but for an authentic purpose.

Their first working model was large, made out of a wet/dry vacuum, a trash can, and PVC pipes that they drilled air holes into. That rudimentary version was big enough to scrub a large volume of air, such as the open spaces in a school building. As they fine-tuned the model, they came up with a household-sized scrubber, effective for cleaning smaller areas. The design process generated mathematics discussions about measuring volume, air flow, and pump rates.

As they prepared to go public with their invention, students had to make marketing decisions about pricing their new product. Local Ace Hardware outlets and a convenience store chain both agreed to sell the product kit at zero markup.

The students' design even impressed civil defense officials, and their U.S. senator introduced the project to the *Congressional Record*. Students gained more attention for the project when the news media came calling. Each connection to an authentic audience recharged students' interest in the project.

As a continuation of the project, Clause and his students plan to run a crowdfunding campaign on Kickstarter to raise money to patent their product. Students are learning firsthand what it takes to get a product from idea to market—including trademark and copyright, intellectual property issues, and product liability. "They're getting a good idea of the whole process," Clause says, "and whether they're ready to bite off something like that [with their next big idea]."

Clause and his students haven't hesitated to jump into their next project. Working with the local transportation department, students are brainstorming how to protect utility poles from lava damage and how to pave over lava in case local roads get destroyed.

"There's a million things to do," the teacher says about finding authentic projects. "Whatever's happening in your community, just glom onto that as a project."

Designing his entire STEM curriculum from scratch takes more effort than using canned materials, Clause admits, "but the quality of the work students produce, and the quality of the reaction you get from them, are phenomenal."

How to Get Started With Entrepreneurship and Innovation Projects

Projects that put students in the innovator role challenge them to use their creativity to come up with novel solutions. This could involve anything from developing a new product to improving a system, such as household recycling. Teach students to use a problem-solving process that they can bring to future situations. For example,

NASA's (2013) engineering design process (which Werberger's students used in the Shark Tank project) outlines a series of steps, from identifying a problem to refining the final solution.

Foster entrepreneurial thinking by giving students authentic opportunities to bring their ideas to market. That doesn't mean projects have to be all about making money. Social entrepreneurship projects challenge students to use business strategies to address social or environmental problems; for example, they may ask, "How can we, as young social entrepreneurs, reduce rates of childhood hunger in our community or another place in the world?"

Resources to teach and encourage entrepreneurship and innovation include the following websites.

- BizWorld.org (http://bizworld.org) offers a trio of ready-made projects that teach students, grades 3–8, the principles of entrepreneurship.

- The Network for Teaching Entrepreneurship (http://nfte.com) sponsors an annual National Youth Entrepreneurship Challenge and offers professional development for teachers.

- Global Entrepreneurship Week (www.gew.co) is an annual, worldwide event that includes activities to encourage young entrepreneurs.

- DECA (www.deca.org) is a nonprofit promoting hands-on learning about entrepreneurship and offers classroom resources for setting up school-based enterprises.

Chapter 5

Media Literacy Projects: Becoming Savvier Consumers and Creators of Media

Do your students know how to send a letter to the editor, comment on an online news story, detect an Internet hoax, or create and publish multimedia content of their own? In our information-rich world, media literacy encompasses an essential skill set necessary for full participation in our democratic society, according to Renee Hobbs (2010), founder of the Media Education Lab and professor of communication studies at the University of Rhode Island.

This kind of literacy doesn't develop just by surrounding yourself with online content or having a Facebook page or Twitter account. Veteran educators Gail Desler and Natalie Bernasconi (2014) compare learning to navigate life online with learning to drive:

> Kids grow up riding around in cars, but that doesn't mean they have the maturity and judgment to get behind the wheel without adult guidance and training.

> Similarly, in the digital world, students need our mod-
> eling and guidance in order to put the rules of the
> road into practice on their journey to becoming full-
> fledged digital citizens. (pp. 10–11)

When teachers design projects to deliberately teach and scaffold students' media literacy skills, students learn to access information from multiple sources, analyze messages in a variety of forms, create their own multimedia content, and perhaps even take social action by sharing knowledge and collaborating to solve meaningful, real-world problems (Hobbs, 2010; Hobbs & Moore, 2013). These expansive life skills establish core citizenship competencies for the digital age (Hobbs, 2010; Hobbs & Moore, 2013).

Media literacy projects can start as early as the elementary grades. Students who are more media aware are primed to ask questions about how media messages aim to influence their behavior. Projects might examine everything from kids' cereal advertisements to toy marketing campaigns.

By middle school, when students are interested in questions of identity, they are likely to take a keen interest in projects about body image. What's real? What's manipulated? How do media portrayals affect how we see ourselves? Those can be compelling departure points for projects.

Even science curricula can be infused with media literacy, according to teacher Chris Sperry (2012). For example, he describes students sorting fact from fiction in films about climate change or analyzing scenes from *CSI* for valid applications of forensic science.

Beyond being savvy media consumers, students can leverage their understanding of media to become more capable content producers themselves. Research about connected learning underscores the importance for 21st century learners to have opportunities to pursue their interests and passions. To do this, they need access to powerful tools for connecting and making meaning (Ito et al., 2013).

Armin Heurich, teacher librarian at Ithaca High School in Ithaca, New York, emphasizes media literacy across content areas. He draws on his background in film and video production when he collaborates with teachers on project design. Before becoming an educator, he was involved in independent filmmaking and public-access cable TV and brings that expertise to K–12 education. He also consults with a media education project called Project Look Sharp.

A few of his examples illustrate the range of project possibilities. Government students analyze political advertising and then produce their own campaign ads. English students create podcasts about their life experiences in the style of the National Public Radio programs *This I Believe* and *This American Life*. Science students apply their understanding of forensics to create crime-solving documentaries.

Across all subject areas, students produce original work that is improved through peer review and critique. Authentic audiences view their final products. "It's critical that students have their work seen and appreciated," Heurich insists. PBL instills "a pride of ownership" that may be lacking, he says, in an assignment that only the teacher sees.

Students who are newcomers to the United States, for example, created videos about their family traditions and cultural heritage. The project not only helped students improve their English language proficiency, but screening their videos for a public audience built a stronger sense of community. "It was a beautiful thing," Heurich says.

Teachers with limited experience in media production may be wary of projects that require students to shoot video or edit soundtracks. But inexperience doesn't have to be a barrier. Students as young as first graders can successfully produce podcasts or create multimedia stories that combine words and images using easy-to-learn digital tools such as VoiceThread (http://voicethread.com) or Storybird (https://storybird.com).

"I'm presuming [at the start of high school projects] that people have no experience with media production," Heurich says. The technologies needed for creating multimedia content have become increasingly easy to use. If students don't already know how to shoot video with their cell phones or edit using iMovie, they tend to pick up the tech skills fast. "It takes little time to develop a relative level of mastery, so the tool gets out of the way for you," Heurich says.

In many classrooms, students who do have experience with multimedia production become the go-to experts, coaching both peers and teachers in the use of digital tools. This opens opportunities for students to bring their talents and strengths into the classroom and for teachers to model being learners themselves.

Instead of focusing on the technology, Heurich recommends emphasizing the more important takeaways of media literacy. That starts with understanding the choices an author has made. "Students hear a lot about being manipulated by media," Heurich says, "but they don't fully comprehend it until they produce media themselves."

He vividly recalls the first time he edited video. "This was back in 1982 or something," Heurich says, "and I remember what it was like to mash it up, play with the soundtrack and voiceover. I spent all night trying different approaches to create new meaning out of existing raw material. I was startled by the power of media—how it can communicate something so effectively and how the message can be different with one editing choice. I've never looked at media as a consumer the same way again."

That's the kind of insight students gain when they ask questions about an author's intent and choice of imagery to convey a message. As students learn more about media-making techniques, they learn to spot those choices when they see a film, television ad, YouTube video, or newscast. Instead of being passive consumers, they become actively engaged audiences ready to ask critical questions, such as, "Why has the director chosen this particular camera angle? What's been edited out of the frame? How does the choice of music influence the listener's emotional experience?"

With close reading of media, students start to expand their own creative toolkits and become more critical content producers themselves. "They start to pay attention to factors like image composition, juxtaposition, color usage, how you layer audio, use of text, font choice, graphic design. Everything does matter," Heurich says. During the making of a thirty-second political campaign ad or a two-minute video scene from *Macbeth*, for example, students "might spend two weeks making subtle changes," he says. Similar to a writers' workshop approach in language arts, students improve their multimedia work through peer critique and with time to produce multiple drafts.

Allowing time for that fine-tuning to happen is an important strategy for project planning. As students reflect on their progress and invite critique from peers, Heurich hears students "engaged in lively discussions. They're unlocking deeper meaning in a self-directed manner. They're able to formulate the questions they want to answer rather than just answering questions."

How to Get Started With Media Literacy Projects

From a young age, students are both consumers and creators of media, from TV and YouTube to digital gaming and social media. Across grade levels, look for project opportunities that call on students to access digital information, critically evaluate it, and produce their own content.

For example, a driving question for a civics project might ask students, "How can we use social media to amplify youth voice in politics?" or in language arts, "How can we make book trailers to convince middle schoolers to check out the books we love?"

Resources for teaching media literacy include the following websites.

- Common Sense Media (www.commonsensemedia.org) helps families make smart media choices and offers educators a curriculum on digital literacy and citizenship.

- The Media Education Lab (http://mediaeducationlab .com), founded by Renee Hobbs, offers multimedia teaching resources and educational programs to promote media literacy.

- The National Association for Media Literacy Education (http://namle.net) curates a resource hub and hosts an annual conference to promote media literacy.

- Project Look Sharp (http://projectlooksharp.org), based at Ithaca College, provides extensive lesson plans and curriculum kits to foster media literacy across curricula and grade levels.

Chapter 6

Storytelling Projects: Cultivating a Strategic Tool

Knowing how to craft a compelling story, a skill that dates back to our cave-dwelling ancestors, has new cachet in the 21st century. A good story can make all the difference in a job interview, on a crowdfunding platform, in a television ad, or in a pitch to investors (Tugend, 2014). Author and executive coach Harrison Monarth (2014), writing in the *Harvard Business Review*, describes storytelling as a *strategic tool*, useful for everything from improving health care outcomes to swaying jurors. As he explains:

> A story can go where quantitative analysis is denied admission: our hearts. Data can persuade people, but it doesn't inspire them to act; to do that, you need to wrap your vision in a story that fires the imagination and stirs the soul. (Monarth, 2014)

Storytelling has always had a home in the classroom, especially among teachers who appreciate the power of a good tale to make learning memorable. Used well, the narrative structure provides a hook for grabbing, and holding, attention.

By the time they reach high school, most students have had considerable practice with deconstructing stories—identifying rising and falling action, analyzing character traits, and distilling literary themes. Those elements are well worth knowing. But the full power of storytelling isn't unleashed unless students have opportunities to be story creators themselves. With access to multimedia tools and online publishing—from video-editing software to comic book creator tools to fan fiction sites—digital learners have expanded opportunities to bring their own stories to authentic audiences.

When digital storytelling is a deliberate focus of PBL, students can create content about a wide range of subjects. They might use storytelling as an advocacy tool if they decide to raise awareness of an issue they have investigated. Elementary students have teamed up with peers from around the world to produce a book about saving endangered species. In other storytelling projects, students have created comics, hosted spoken-word events and poetry slams, and screened their own movies at red-carpet events to share their work with audiences.

Heather Wolpert-Gawron, a middle school language arts teacher and active blogger from California (known online as @tweenteacher), taps the power of stories to help her students recognize their own potential as world changers. As she explains, "Our whole lives are intertwined with stories. We have to recognize our own themes if we're going to live by them. What are our mottos? What are the meanings of our lives? Someone's not going to just hand that to you—you have to be able to recognize the story you're living."

Wolpert-Gawron sees strong parallels between her roles as educator and storyteller. "When I design curriculum, I'm telling the story of my students' academic life during the school year," she says. A well-designed project follows its own narrative arc, with students cast as protagonists in their own learning adventure.

How might a storytelling project unfold? Let's listen to Wolpert-Gawron deconstruct a project about superheroes (and much more).

Like all good projects, this one begins with a brief but intriguing entry event to fire up student inquiry. Early in the school year, Wolpert-Gawron shows students a short video that she made using iMovie. "It challenges them to think about, 'What is a hero? What is service? If you were a superhero, would your superpower be a blessing or a curse?' Then it ends with this dramatic message: all you need are the powers of an eighth grader to tell your tale!"

The superhero theme is perennially popular with students. "It's a silver bullet," Wolpert-Gawron says, for earning middle schoolers' attention. As a project focus, creating superhero stories offers a compelling way to introduce the hero's journey theme in literature and sets the stage for a wide range of other language arts activities. Rather than feeling like a series of disconnected assignments, these project components are woven together by the driving question, How can we create superheroes who use their powers to improve the world?

With students on board after the entry event, the teacher moves into writing origin stories. Having students craft a backstory about their superhero builds more student buy-in for the project. "If they can't get into that character," Wolpert-Gawron says, "they can't have ownership of the superhero's passions and causes. And that's going to be important later when we get into advocacy."

By the end of the project, students will speak in the persona (and costume) of their superhero characters about the global issues that they want to solve. In the process, they will apply their understanding of persuasive writing techniques, draw on media sources to understand current issues, write convincingly about science concepts, and meet a range of other Common Core–aligned standards.

The veteran language arts teacher incorporates a variety of strategies to help students develop their characters and story lines. For example, she teaches plot development using Hemingway's classic six-word short story: "For sale: baby shoes, never worn." In this activity, students write a six-word story in this style.

Students add more details when they create visuals of their superheroes. Online cartooning, drawing tools, and even photo manipulation can help students who lack confidence in their freehand skills. Wolpert-Gawron also recommends the Create Your Own Superhero activity at Marvel (n.d.).

Character development continues with a graphic organizer activity and then branches off in new directions through the teacher's prompts and probing questions. "By the end of this activity, they're able to answer so many questions about their character that they hadn't thought of before," she says.

To weave nonfiction writing into the project, students investigate the science of superheroes, starting with a TED-Ed series of videos on that topic. "That gets them thinking about the science necessary to seed their stories," she explains. In parallel, students use independent reading time to explore the genre of science fiction and do Internet research to learn more about science concepts that interest them.

Wolpert-Gawron scaffolds instruction as needed to make sure all students understand key concepts, such as the elements of story structure, the importance of sensory detail in narrative, and how to search online and cite sources properly. Scaffolding makes the project accessible to diverse learners, from struggling students to those identified as gifted. "They're all doing the same project," she says.

Midway through the project, as students investigate the science of superpowers, Wolpert-Gawron brings in some outside expertise. A series of phone calls led her to Spyridon Michalakis, a quantum physicist at Caltech. As Wolpert-Gawron (2014) explains in a post for Edutopia:

> Besides having a name that, in itself, could have come straight out of the pages of a comic book, Spiros (as

the kids could call him) himself has the perfect origin story. After all, he is a quantum physicist by day and a consultant on the new Marvel comic movie, *Ant-man*, by night. Perhaps I exaggerate, but the fact that he inspired my students, enriched their fact-based stories, and injected them with new enthusiasm for their characters, surely indicates a latent superpower.

The timing for his visit couldn't have been better, Wolpert-Gawron says. "Students have done the story structure by now. They need to add richness of detail, specifically about the science that created their characters' superpowers." The visiting scientist inspired them with research stories. Later, as students expand their story drafts with scientifically accurate details, they can see how the revision process yields richer, more compelling narratives.

Before the project reaches its conclusion, Wolpert-Gawron also incorporates informational writing by having students prepare news stories that chronicle *sightings* of their superheroes. "They recognize that this is a different style of storytelling," the teacher explains. The news accounts have to be consistent with the characters they have created. "They know their characters so well by now. They can be accurate when it comes to what they would and wouldn't do in public. Would they run? Fly away? Speak to a crowd? What would the witness accounts say?" Some students get creative with visuals, creating blurry photo effects of superhero sightings and posting them to their own Weebly (www.weebly.com) pages.

Finally, it's time for the culminating event: persuasive speeches, in costume and with multimedia visuals, to a United Nations–style assemblage including fellow students and some outside visitors. Students-as-superheroes make their pitches about solving global issues that concern them. The audience weighs arguments and evidence using a Twitter backchannel for real-time discussions and asking probing questions to dig deeper into the speakers' positions. Eventually, the audience selects one argument as the most deserving of UN support.

In a final reflection for the project, Wolpert-Gawron challenges students to bring heroic attributes into their own lives and communities. "The theme of this project isn't just *What is a hero?* but *What is service?* I want them to be able to look back and say, 'How have I been heroic?'" To nudge students in that direction, Wolpert-Gawron once again taps her own narrative powers. "I tell them, 'I get to see the best in you. You show me the beautiful stories that you are. Are other people seeing the themes of your life? Don't be afraid to share the stories that let people see your heart.'"

See *DIY Project Based Learning for ELA and History* (Wolpert-Gawron, 2015) for more detail on the superhero project.

How to Get Started With Storytelling Projects

Stories are such an inextricable part of learning that we can take them for granted. Projects that specifically emphasize storytelling remind students of the components of good narrative and challenge them to use all the tools at their disposal to create memorable tales of their own.

Some resources to help include the following websites.

- The Center for Digital Storytelling (http://storycenter .org) features examples of first-person stories on a wide range of themes, from the refugee experience to community building to youth activism. See how storytelling can be a tool for change.

- *Digital Is* (http://digitalis.nwp.org), from the National Writing Project, provides a platform for educators to think aloud about the roles of connected writing and storytelling in the digital age.

- Mapping Media to the Curriculum (http://maps .playingwithmedia.com), the website of digital media expert and author Wesley Fryer (who blogs at *Moving at the Speed of Creativity*), offers an online guide to digital media creation tools for producing everything from five-photo stories to radio shows.

- Youth Voices (http://youthvoices.net) is a platform for publishing student writing, including multimedia content, and connecting young writers. Student storytellers can find an authentic audience for their work here.

Chapter 7
Project-Based Learning Challenges

Each of the projects described in the previous pages represents a significant investment by the teachers who designed and facilitated these innovative learning experiences. Although these were successful projects by many measures, they didn't come without challenges. At the outset, teachers wondered, "Will students seize the opportunity to learn in new ways, using unfamiliar technologies and connecting with people outside the comfort zone of their classroom? Can students manage more of their own learning and collaborate effectively with peers? Will they really learn what they need to know when given more voice and choice about their own education?"

PBL teachers don't let potential worries derail projects that are rife with possibilities for rich learning. Instead, they anticipate challenges and respond with troubleshooting strategies. In the process, they model for their students what it means to be an agile, resourceful, adaptable learner.

Let's consider a few common PBL challenges and solutions.

What About Content Coverage?

When teachers first consider a shift to PBL, one of their most frequently voiced concerns has to do with time for content coverage. "We'd like to offer our students these real-world project experiences," they often say, "but we have to use class time to cover required content and prepare for standardized tests. There's just no time left for projects."

The best way to tackle this concern is to revisit the core ideas of PBL described previously (see page 7). Take another look at that first point: "The inquiry project, framed by a driving question, is the centerpiece of instruction. It's not an add-on or hands-on activity wrapping up a unit of study. Instead, the project is designed with specific learning goals in mind" (Boss & Krauss, 2014). Now think again about the project examples you have just read, paying attention to the academic content that's woven into these PBL experiences. In the Shark Tank project, for instance, students learned specific language arts content alongside STEM concepts. Humanities teacher Raleigh Werberger pointed out students' purposefulness, whether they were reading a biography of Steve Jobs or learning to write persuasive pitches.

PBL doesn't mean putting more demands on the schedule; it means using learning time differently. Think of PBL as a *yes–and* proposition: projects address important academic content in depth (that's the *yes*) *and* create meaningful, relevant opportunities for students to acquire the new skills and literacies they need. If that's too hard to imagine, see if you can visit a class while a project is underway, and listen to students grapple with important concepts. Or, better yet, attend a culminating event where students share their understanding and work products. Ask them about what they gain from doing rigorous, relevant PBL.

Even with assurance that they aren't throwing content to the wind, teachers may still feel as if they are taking a big leap by replacing tried-and-true, textbook-based instruction with projects that don't follow a script or come with a daily lesson plan. There's no shame in borrowing or adapting a standards-aligned project plan that has already been classroom tested. In fact, many teachers find this to be a helpful first step into PBL. (See the PBL resources on page 61 for information about project libraries.)

When teachers feel ready to move ahead with their own project designs, it's worth taking a fresh look at those content standards. What are the big ideas of their discipline? How do those ideas connect to the world beyond the classroom? Good projects don't just *cover* content; they "make content standards relevant. That makes learning more purposeful and concepts more memorable for students" (Boss, 2014c).

How Do We Connect With Outside Experts?

Several of the examples in this book mention the role of experts from outside the classroom. From the physicist who inspired superhero stories to the makerspace volunteers who shared their know-how for the Shark Tank session, experts expand on the content knowledge that teachers possess. They also bring insights from the workplace, providing students with windows into emerging career fields.

In some cases, the tables are turned, and adults ask students for help solving community concerns. Students can't help but feel more engaged in learning when they see that their work is being taken seriously by community members.

How do teachers make connections to community experts? How can they help students look beyond the classroom to identify problems worth solving?

Heather Wolpert-Gawron recommends that teachers start with their own friends and colleagues and put out the word. "Tap your network," she says. Her connection with the physicist, for example, came about because she called a friend who happened to work at Caltech. She was specific about what she was looking for in an expert. "I wanted to find someone who could talk about science in a way that middle school students could understand," Wolpert-Gawron says. She was also flexible about how they might connect. An in-person visit was ideal, but she was open to a Skype call if that was more convenient. Before inviting the scientist to her classroom, she arranged a meeting to brief him on the project. And before he showed up in class, she also prepared her eighth graders to be ready with good questions. These strategies help to make an expert's time focused. In many instances, experts become allies, returning for students' final presentations and talking up their positive classroom experience with colleagues. "You've got to get the good work of our schools out there. Just step up and do it," she says.

For several of the projects described previously, students needed access to data to get a better understanding of community issues. Montana teacher Gail Shatkus has found that connecting students with adult community members—the *keepers* of data—is one of the great values of GIS projects. "Students become on a par [with adults]," she says. Gaining the confidence to call a state engineer for data or present results to the county commission doesn't happen overnight. "Like any mentoring relationship, you start out side by side with students. Gradually, you give them more and more responsibility. Eventually, they go and collect the data themselves. They make the calls."

Robert Kolvoord, with Virginia's Geospatial Semester program, has seen many productive collaborations between students and community organizations. Students have done habitat mapping for fish and wildlife agencies, analyzed historical data to locate Civil War–era battlements, and analyzed local watersheds for a conservation organization. These projects become true partnerships, with students contributing something valuable to the community organizations. In many instances, organizations don't have the capacity or time to do the data analysis that students can deliver. Students may need coaching to learn how to work well with adults—and the reverse is also true, Kolvoord acknowledges. That's all part of a teacher's role as a project facilitator and mentor.

Connecting students with community partners and content experts does take time and effort, but it doesn't all have to come from the teacher. Parent volunteers can be enlisted to help track down experts, some of whom may be parents themselves. (Hint: Build a database of content experts so you won't have to start from scratch with each project.)

As students get more accustomed to learning through PBL, they start to develop their own strategies for locating the experts or community partners they need. They develop a knack for networking—a valuable skill for everyone from politicians to entrepreneurs to community activists. "The contact lists that some of our students have in their cell phones would amaze you," Shatkus says.

How Do We Manage the Messy Learning That Happens in PBL?

If you were to walk into any of the classrooms described in the previous examples, what would you expect to see? It's unlikely that you'd find students sitting quietly, listening to the teacher lecture from a textbook. Although you might notice brief periods of direct instruction, you would be more apt to find students working in small teams, doing independent work online, or perhaps leaving the classroom altogether to conduct research. Alongside the teacher, you might notice other adults contributing to discussions or getting interviewed by students.

"Learning is a messy process—and authentic, project-based learning immerses us in unique parts of this mess," reflects Joshua Block (2014), a humanities teacher at Science Leadership Academy in Philadelphia. The challenge facing teachers is how to make sure this mess has a purposefulness that results in deep learning.

Block (2014) elaborates on his approach to managing PBL:

> Understanding the need for messiness, I attempt to structure class periods accordingly. The beginning of units and the final stages of projects are either times when we work as a unified class, or times when students and groups focus on specific, clearly defined tasks. Our goals are to establish background understanding of a topic or to bring their project-based work to fruition. I plan these days so that everyone has clearly defined tasks to complete.

Similarly, Wolpert-Gawron provides her middle schoolers with calendars and checklists for milestone assignments along the project path. As she explains, "Some students want to see one week at a time. What's due when? I post that on our class website. Others want to see where the whole project is heading, from beginning to end. I'll talk them through that. And some just want to think about a day at a time. I give them a daily agenda."

Clearly, there's a deliberate plan behind these projects, even if the day-to-day vibe feels pretty loose. Advance planning is detailed enough so that teachers can anticipate challenges ahead but also flexible enough to make adjustments on the fly.

Make the most of messy learning by planning for the following factors.

- **Learning goals:** Define learning goals at the outset. What will students know and be able to do by the end of the project? How can you chunk these learning goals into manageable pieces? Which teaching strategies will you incorporate, and when, to help students develop understanding? Backward planning is key for ensuring that the project experiences add up to meaningful learning.

- **Teamwork:** If students are going to work in project teams, have a game plan for collaboration. Ask yourself at the project design stage, "Why does this project require collaboration?" It might involve complex challenges, requiring students to specialize, much as project teams operate in the world outside the classroom. Or perhaps you want to give students the opportunity to work from their strengths or interests. The Shark Tank project, for instance, had students self-identify as engineers, contractors, and other roles, based on their strengths.

Once teams are up and running, don't assume that effective collaboration will happen automatically. You may need to teach students strategies for reaching a consensus, managing conflict, and providing effective peer critique. Plan for regular team check-ins to make sure teams are working well together, and be ready to intervene if they need help getting back on track.

- **Self-management:** If students have had few opportunities to manage their own learning, they may feel adrift in an open-ended project environment that invites them to make choices. Help them learn to set their own learning goals, manage their time effectively, and develop the persistence that will help them succeed not only in PBL but in life.

What Does Assessment Look Like in PBL?

At the project planning stage, you identify learning goals and anticipate the teaching and learning activities that will help students reach understanding. This is also the time to consider assessment strategies. In a summative assessment, how will students show what they know and can do? And how can you leverage formative assessment throughout the project to tap into students' thinking, address misunderstandings, and guide students toward deeper learning?

Assessment is an ongoing process in PBL, from project kickoff until the culminating event and then post-project reflection. At the project launch, a teacher observes and listens to student conversations for evidence of curiosity. Are students asking questions? Do they appear motivated and eager to dive in? Early in the project, a variety of strategies—including concept maps, know-wonder-learn charts, online surveys, and whole-class discussions—will help you discover what prior knowledge students bring to the topic.

In the messy middle, formative assessment is ongoing—exit slips or quick writes to check for understanding, Socratic seminars to foster critical thinking, and research proposals to give insight into how students are anticipating their next steps. Student blog posts offer another way to hear students think through their learning process as well as a format for engaging with them via comments.

As students begin to apply their understanding to produce original work, you might review storyboards for videos or offer feedback on rough drafts of written work. Formative feedback doesn't all have to come from the teacher, either. Peer review or critiques by content experts offer more opportunities for students to get feedback on their work in progress.

Most importantly, make sure that students have time to make good use of this feedback. Allow time in the project calendar for them to produce multiple drafts or prototypes. This is the *secret sauce* of PBL, leading to high-quality final work that students will be eager to present publicly.

Takeaways and Reflections

Digital-age PBL offers a promising antidote for the lack of engagement that keeps too many of our students from pursuing the meaningful, motivating education that they deserve.

Emotional engagement doesn't always get top billing in discussions of school change, but it may be the most critical factor for improving the current picture. The same Gallup (2014) report that documents the dispiriting decline in student optimism describes emotional engagement as "the heartbeat of the education process, pumping energy and imagination into students' day-to-day experiences at school" (p. 16). Furthermore, the report points out the direct link between engagement and academic performance.

To meet new learning goals, school change expert Michael Fullan calls on us to rethink how students and teachers work together. The model he envisions has "teachers as partners in learning with students, accelerated by technology" (Fullan & Langworthy, 2013, p. 11). Their shared inquiry should be "steeped in real-life problem solving" (Fullan, 2013, p. 33). As we've heard in example after example, this is an accurate description of the learning that unfolds in digital-age PBL.

Heidi Hayes Jacobs (2014) encourages us to rethink education with a focus on three important literacies: (1) digital, (2) media, and (3) global. You have heard about projects that integrate digital tools, build media literacy, and set the stage for students to engage with problems affecting the world beyond the classroom. Some projects push the boundaries of what students can do even further, using emerging technologies as an entrée to interesting new fields. At the same time, PBL reinforces the foundational literacies that will always be evergreen.

In significant ways, PBL changes the dynamics between teacher and student. Rather than wondering how education will apply to their lives, students are invited to bring their talents and current interests to projects. If they have a desire to make a difference in their community or in the larger world, they don't have to wait until a vague-sounding *someday* to get busy making change happen. They can apply what they know today. Better yet, adults from both inside and outside the classroom are ready to encourage their efforts and provide the best kind of assessment: appreciation for work well done.

PBL Resources

The following books, online resources, and project libraries provide in-depth strategies for planning and facilitating project-based learning for digital-age learners. Visit **go.solution-tree.com /technology** to access materials related to this book.

Books

Boss, S., & Krauss, J. (2014). *Reinventing project-based learning: Your field guide to real-world projects in the digital age* (2nd ed.). Eugene, OR: International Society for Technology in Education.

Ferriter, W. M., & Garry, A. (2015). *Teaching the iGeneration: 5 easy ways to introduce essential skills with web 2.0 tools* (2nd ed.). Bloomington, IN: Solution Tree Press.

Krauss, J., & Boss, S. (2013). *Thinking through project-based learning: Guiding deeper inquiry.* Thousand Oaks, CA: Corwin Press.

Larmer, J., Mergendoller, J., & Boss, S. (in press). *Setting the standard for project-based learning: A proven approach to rigorous classroom instruction.* Alexandria, VA: Association for Supervision and Curriculum Development.

Larmer, J., Ross, D., & Mergendoller, J. R. (2009). *PBL starter kit: To-the-point advice, tools and tips for your first project.* Novato, CA: Buck Institute for Education.

Online Resources

- **Buck Institute for Education (http://bie.org):** The Buck Institute for Education promotes PBL to improve 21st century teaching and learning. This nonprofit organization maintains an extensive online library (http://bie.org/project_search) of sample project plans and videos and offers downloadable tools for project planning, management, and assessment.

- **Edutopia (www.edutopia.org):** Produced by the George Lucas Educational Foundation, Edutopia promotes PBL as a key strategy to improve teaching and learning. The website includes an extensive library of videos, articles, blogs, research summaries, classroom guides, and online communities where educators can connect and seek advice.

Project Libraries

In addition to the Buck Institute for Education's project library, more examples of classroom-tested projects can be found at the following websites.

- Expeditionary Learning Center for Student Work (http://centerforstudentwork.elschools.org)

- Envision Schools Project Exchange (http://envisionprojects.org/pub/docs/envision/index.htm)

- Project Based Learning University (http://pblu.org)

- Projects at High Tech High (http://hightechhigh.org/projects)

- The Project Approach (http://projectapproach.org)

References and Resources

American Statistical Association. (2010). Free K–12 statistics education resources. *The Statistics Teacher Network, 76,* 4.

Block, J. (2014, January 7). *Embracing messy learning* [Web log post]. Accessed at www.edutopia.org/blog/embracing-messy-learning -joshua-block on January 12, 2015.

Boss, S. (2012). *Bringing innovation to school: Empowering students to thrive in a changing world.* Bloomington, IN: Solution Tree Press.

Boss, S. (2013). *PBL for 21st century success: Teaching critical thinking, collaboration, communication, and creativity.* Novato, CA: Buck Institute for Education.

Boss, S. (2014a, May 20). *How to help your students develop data literacy* [Web log post]. Accessed at www.edutopia.org/blog /helping-students-develop-digital-literacy-suzie-boss on January 12, 2015.

Boss, S. (2014b, March 31). *Students put global skills to work* [Web log post]. Accessed at www.edutopia.org/blog/students-put-global -skills-to-work-suzie-boss on January 12, 2015.

Boss, S. (2014c, October 17). *Time to debunk those PBL myths* [Web log post]. Accessed at www.edutopia.org/blog/time-debunk-those -pbl-myths-suzie-boss on January 12, 2015.

Boss, S., & Krauss, J. (2014). *Reinventing project-based learning: Your field guide to real-world projects in the digital age* (2nd ed.). Eugene, OR: International Society for Technology in Education.

Desler, G., & Bernasconi, N. (2014). Driving without a license: Digital writing without digital citizenship. In R. E. Ferdig, T. V. Rasinski, & K. E. Pytash (Eds.), *Using technology to enhance writing: Innovative approaches to literacy instruction* (pp. 9–18). Bloomington, IN: Solution Tree Press.

Edelson, D. C. (2013). *Geo-education: Essential preparation for an interconnected world*. Washington, DC: National Geographic Society. Accessed at http://education.nationalgeographic.com/education/geo-education-essential-preparation-interconnected-world/?ar_a=1 on January 12, 2015.

Education Development Center Oceans of Data Institute. (n.d.a). *The common online data analysis platform (CODAP)*. Accessed at http://oceansofdata.org/projects/common-online-data-analysis-platform-codap on January 12, 2015.

Education Development Center Oceans of Data Institute. (n.d.b). *The data landscape*. Accessed at http://oceansofdata.org/data-landscape on January 12, 2015.

Ferriter, W. M., & Garry, A. (2015). *Teaching the iGeneration: 5 easy ways to introduce essential skills with web 2.0 tools* (2nd ed.). Bloomington, IN: Solution Tree Press.

Finkelstein, N., Hanson, T., Huang, C.-W., Hirschman, B., & Huang, M. (2010). *Effects of problem based economics on high school economics instruction* (NCEE 2010–4002). Washington, DC: National Center for Education Evaluation and Regional Assistance, Institute of Education Sciences, U.S. Department of Education.

Fullan, M. (2013). *Stratosphere: Integrating technology, pedagogy, and change knowledge*. Toronto, Ontario, Canada: Pearson.

Fullan, M., & Donnelly, K. (2013). *Alive in the swamp: Assessing digital innovations in education*. London: Nesta.

Fullan, M., & Langworthy, M. (2013). *Towards a new end: New pedagogies for deep learning*. Seattle, WA: Collaborative Impact.

Gallup. (2014). *State of America's schools: The path to winning again in education*. Washington, DC: Author.

Hobbs, R. (2010). *Digital and media literacy: A plan of action.* Washington, DC: Aspen Institute Communications and Society Program.

Hobbs, R., & Moore, D. C. (2013). *Discovering media literacy: Teaching digital media and popular culture in elementary school.* Thousand Oaks, CA: Corwin Press.

Isaacson, W. (2011). *Steve Jobs.* New York: Simon & Schuster.

Ito, M., Gutiérrez, K., Livingstone, S., Penuel, B., Rhodes, J., Salen, K., et al. (2013). *Connected learning: An agenda for research and design.* Irvine, CA: Digital Media and Learning Research Hub.

Jacobs, H. H. (Ed.). (2014). *Leading the new literacies.* Bloomington, IN: Solution Tree Press.

Krauss, J., & Boss, S. (2013). *Thinking through project-based learning: Guiding deeper inquiry.* Thousand Oaks, CA: Corwin Press.

Larmer, J., Mergendoller, J., & Boss, S. (in press). *Setting the standard for project-based learning: A proven approach to rigorous classroom instruction.* Alexandria, VA: Association for Supervision and Curriculum Development.

Larmer, J., Ross, D., & Mergendoller, J. R. (2009). *PBL starter kit: To-the-point advice, tools and tips for your first project.* Novato, CA: Buck Institute for Education.

Lenz, B. (2014, October 23). *New evidence: Deeper learning improves student outcomes* [Web log post]. Accessed at www.edutopia.org/blog/new-evidence-deeper-learning-improves-student-outcomes-bob-lenz on January 12, 2015.

Marvel. (n.d.). *Create your own superhero.* Accessed at http://marvel.com/games/play/31/create_your_own_superhero on January 12, 2015.

Mergendoller, J. R., Maxwell, N. L., & Bellisimo, Y. (2006). The effectiveness of problem-based instruction: A comparative study of instructional methods and student characteristics. *Interdisciplinary Journal of Problem-Based Learning, 1*(2), 49–69.

Monarth, H. (2014, March 11). The irresistible power of storytelling as a strategic business tool. *Harvard Business Review*. Accessed at https://hbr.org/2014/03/the-irresistible-power-of-storytelling-as-a-strategic-business-tool on January 12, 2015.

NASA. (2013, November 3). *Engineering design process*. Accessed at www.nasa.gov/audience/foreducators/plantgrowth/reference/Eng_Design_5–12.html#.VL1u7kfF8xO on January 12, 2015.

Network for Teaching Entrepreneurship. (n.d.). *Our impact*. Accessed at http://nfte.com/pages/our-impact on January 12, 2015.

New Tech Network. (2014). *Global Happiness Project—Phase three: Reflect & advocate*. Accessed at https://docs.google.com/document/d/18IeQAssmj0vqYkPDVhWchefR63BQ5RzEPzYjQzg6_IU/edit?pli=1# on January 29, 2015.

Prosek, J. (2009). *Bird, butterfly, eel*. New York: Simon & Schuster.

Schulten, K. (2010, August 23). *Teaching with infographics: Places to start* [Web log post]. Accessed at http://learning.blogs.nytimes.com/2010/08/23/teaching-with-infographics-places-to-start/?_r=0 on January 12, 2015.

Sperry, C. (2012). Teaching critical thinking through media literacy. *Science Scope, 35*(9), 45–49.

Steinbeck, J. (1939). *The grapes of wrath*. New York: Viking Press.

Stites, R. (1998). *Evaluation of project-based learning: What does research say about outcomes from project-based learning?* Redwood City, CA: San Mateo County Office of Education.

Thomas, J. W. (2000). *A review of research on project-based learning*. San Rafael, CA: Autodesk Foundation. Accessed at http://bobpearlman.org/BestPractices/PBL_Research.pdf on January 12, 2015.

Tugend, A. (2014, December 12). Storytelling your way to a better job or a stronger start-up. *New York Times*. Accessed at www.nytimes.com/2014/12/13/your-money/storytelling-to-find-a-job-or-build-a-business.html?_r=0 on January 12, 2015.

Vega, V. (2012, December 3). *Project-based learning research review.* Accessed at www.edutopia.org/pbl-research-learning-outcomes on January 12, 2015.

Werberger, R. (2014, June 10). *Using entrepreneurship to transform student work* [Web log post]. Accessed at www.edutopia.org/blog /pbl-entrepreneurship-transforms-student-work-raleigh-werberger on January 12, 2015.

Wolpert-Gawron, H. (2014, October 30). *STEM and writing: A super combination* [Web log post]. Accessed at www.edutopia.org/blog /stem-and-writing-super-combination-heather-wolpert-gawron on January 12, 2015.

Wolpert-Gawron, H. (2015). *DIY project based learning for ELA and history.* New York: Routledge.

Zeiser, K. L., Taylor, J., Rickles, J., Garet, M. S., & Segeritz, M. (2014). *Evidence of deeper learning outcomes* (Report 3. Findings From the Study of Deeper Learning: Opportunities and Outcomes). Washington, DC: American Institutes for Research. Accessed at www.air.org/sites/default/files/downloads/report/Report_3 _Evidence_of_Deeper_Learning_Outcomes.pdf on January 12, 2015.

Zhao, Y. (2012). *World class learners: Educating creative and entrepreneurial students.* Thousand Oaks, CA: Corwin Press.

Zhao, Y. (2014). *Who's afraid of the big bad dragon? Why China has the best (and worst) education system in the world.* San Francisco: Jossey-Bass.

Solutions for Digital Learner–Centered Classrooms

The *Solutions Series* offers practitioners easy-to-implement recommendations on each book's topic—professional learning communities, digital classrooms, or modern learning. In a short, reader-friendly format, these how-to guides equip K–12 educators with the tools they need to take their school or district to the next level.

Designing Teacher-Student Partnership Classrooms
Meg Ormiston
BKF680

Evaluating and Assessing Tools in the Digital Swamp
Michael Fullan and Katelyn Donnelly
BKF636

From Master Teacher to Master Learner
Will Richardson
BKF679

Creating Purpose-Driven Learning Experiences
William M. Ferriter
BKF691

Using Digital Games as Assessment and Instruction Tools
Ryan L. Schaaf
BKF666

Inspiring Creativity and Innovation in K–12
Douglas Reeves
BKF664